ZEN DOGS

ZEN DOGS

ALEX CEARNS

HarperOne
An Imprint of HarperCollinsPublishers

HarperCollins books may be purchased for educational, business, or sales promotional use. For information please e-mail the Special Markets Department at SPsales@harpercollins.com.

HarperCollins website: http://www.harpercollins.com

FIRST EDITION

Designed by Terry McGrath

ISBN 978-0-06-245937-4

17 18 19 20 SCP 10 9 8 7 6 5 4 3 2

To the dogs of the world. We can learn so much from you when we have open minds and hearts.

CONTENTS

INTRODUCTION

As a pet and wildlife photographer, my job is my lifestyle and my world is all about animals. I love every creature I meet, but dogs are my absolute favorite. Throughout my life, dogs have been great friends and cherished family members. Every day I'm inspired by their boundless ability to fill the world with joy and unconditional love. Their incredible generosity, responsiveness, and sense of fun make them ideal to photograph.

I've had just about every kind of dog in my studio, each endlessly expressive and utterly unique. A few years ago, I captured a particularly compelling moment with a most gorgeous shar-pei, Suzi. Her closed eyes and wide, contented smile suggested calm, euphoric bliss. I called the image *Zen Dog,* and her humans were delighted with the shot.

That photo of Suzi inspired me to capture Zen moments with other dogs. I looked for an expression of spontaneous canine bliss: eyes gently closed, body relaxed, and spirit totally carefree. I discovered that the blink happens in a split second, but truly Zen-worthy expressions happen only when my subject and I are in sync. In that moment nothing else matters. It's pure, unadulterated joy. I also discovered that, in that split second, the dog's distinctive personality—playful, placid, or confident—shines through.

As an animal lover, seeing blissful dogs always brings a smile to my face, and I know I'm not alone. It's even more poignant for me when I know my subject has come from a difficult background. I'm very passionate about animal rescue, and some of the dogs included here experienced hard times before finding their forever homes.

I feel very fortunate to have been united with my two rescue dogs, Pip and Pixel. Found wandering the streets as a twelve-week-old puppy, Pip was severely undernourished. With the help of GreyhoundAngels of Western Australia and a loving foster family, Pip regained her strength and stole my heart at first sight. Pixel was surrendered to Brightside Farm Sanctuary when she was a tiny greyhound puppy. She was a gift to me from the founder of the sanctuary—possibly the best gift I've ever received. Pixel has become a wonderful ambassador for greyhound rescue, appearing in magazines, books, and TV spots. Pip and Pixel even have their own Facebook page, Black Beetle, which has thousands of followers.

Every day my dogs help me to appreciate the simple things in life. Research has found that owning a dog can lower blood pressure, reduce stress hormones, and boost levels of feel-good chemicals in the brain, but every dog lover knows the benefits are far too many to list. I hope this series of images is a gentle and positive reminder of the peace, calm, and joy that dogs bring to our lives. Like the dogs in these photos and the canine companion on your couch, we all need to stop, take a break, relax, and unwind—to breathe it all in and be fully present in each and every experience.

—*Alex Cearns*

ZEN DOGS

Tension is who you think you should be.
Relaxation is who you are.

—CHINESE PROVERB

Harrison, DACHSHUND

Jet, BORDER COLLIE

Barney, KING CHARLES CAVALIER

Bailey, LABRADOR

Kono, MINIATURE POODLE

Very little is needed to make a happy life.

—MARCUS AURELIUS

Kato, AMERICAN STAFFORDSHIRE TERRIER

Hades, CHIHUAHUA

Dayzee, BULLMASTIFF

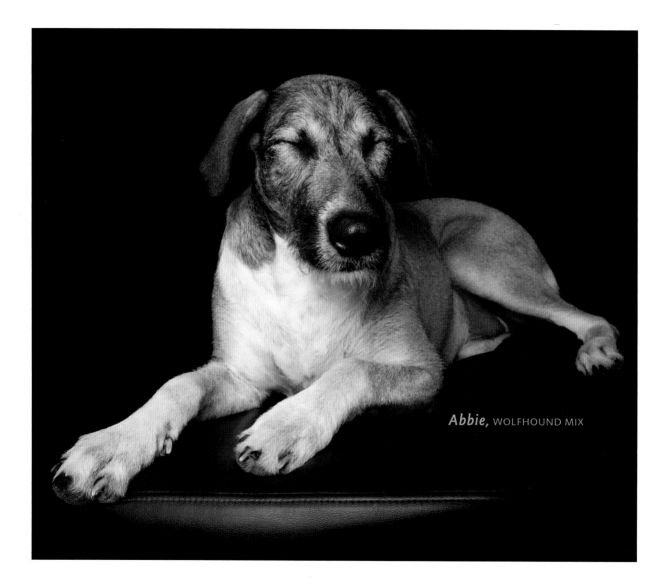

Abbie, WOLFHOUND MIX

Jessie, SHOLLIE

Nothing is left to you at this moment but to have a good laugh.

—CHINESE ZEN MASTER

Minnie, STAFFORDSHIRE BULL TERRIER

Mr. Scruffy, MIXED BREED

Polly, STAFFORDSHIRE BULL TERRIER MIX

Dozer, ROTTWEILER

Abbey, STANDARD POODLE

The question is not what you look at, but what you see.

—HENRY DAVID THOREAU

Muska, HUNGARIAN VIZSLA

Bosco, RED CLOUD KELPIE

Pepperoni, DACHSHUND

Lexie, GREYHOUND MIX

Miley, PUG

You should sit in meditation for twenty minutes a day,
unless you're too busy. Then you should sit for an hour.

—ZEN PROVERB

Jessie, DACHSHUND

Suzi, SHAR-PEI

Butch, BRITTANY

Lily, KELPIE / HUNTAWAY MIX

Daisy, POMERANIAN

There is more to life than increasing its speed.

—GANDHI

Simon, KELPIE MIX

Ollie, STAFFORDSHIRE BULL TERRIER

Bubba, AMERICAN STAFFORDSHIRE TERRIER

Donnie, KELPIE MIX

Sydney, AUSTRALIAN TERRIER

*If you are unable to find the truth right where you are,
where else do you expect to find it?*

—DOGEN

Ned, BORDER COLLIE

Staiton, BULL TERRIER MIX

Bo, KELPIE MIX

Pluto, LABRADOR

Woody, MASTIFF MIX

The pursuit, even of the best things, ought to be calm and tranquil.

—MARCUS TULLIUS CICERO

Kelcie, AIREDALE

Mollie Moo, WOLFHOUND / RETRIEVER MIX

Hunter, LABRADOR MIX

Koda, GERMAN SHEPHERD

Peace is always beautiful.

—WALT WHITMAN

Grover, LABRADOR

Bella, STAFFORDSHIRE BULL TERRIER MIX

Bailey, AUSTRALIAN SHEPHERD

Frasier, HIGHLAND MALTESE

Bailey, BEAGLE

Every situation—nay, every moment—is of infinite worth;
for it is the representative of a whole eternity.

—JOHANN WOLFGANG VON GOETHE

Fred, BASSET HOUND

Chief, GERMAN SHEPHERD

Major, WHITE SHEPHERD

Tatu, RHODESIAN RIDGEBACK

Dolly, AMERICAN STAFFORDSHIRE TERRIER

May all beings have happy minds.

—BUDDHA

Teddy Bear, KELPIE

Lexie, WEIMARANER

Jeffrey, SCHNAUZER

Sidney, BORDER COLLIE

Nothing can bring you peace but yourself.

—RALPH WALDO EMERSON

Harley, BORDER COLLIE MIX

Storm, SIBERIAN HUSKY

Harry, JACKHUAHUA

Pip, GREYHOUND / KELPIE MIX

Boo, BULL TERRIER MIX

*Only when you can be extremely pliable and soft
can you be extremely hard and strong.*

—ZEN PROVERB

Sharon, GOLDEN RETRIEVER MIX

Ben, WOLFHOUND MIX

Peaches, FRENCH BULLDOG

The tighter you squeeze, the less you have.

—THOMAS MERTON

Cooch, KELPIE / ROTTWEILER MIX

Gordon, GREYHOUND

Hairy, CHIHUAHUA / MINIATURE PINSCHER MIX

Gracie, BULL TERRIER MIX

If you're always racing to the next moment,
what happens to the one you're in?

—UNKNOWN

Dug, LABRADOR

Levi, AMERICAN STAFFORDSHIRE TERRIER

Pixel, GREYHOUND

Indy, STAFFORDSHIRE BULL TERRIER

Remember then: there is only one time that is important—Now! It is the most important time because it is the only time when we have any power.

—LEO TOLSTOY

Gem, KELPIE MIX

Effi, WHIPPET

George, GREYHOUND

Andromache, SIBERIAN HUSKY

Zac, KELPIE MIX

Where there is peace and meditation, there is neither anxiety nor doubt.

—ST. FRANCIS OF ASSISI

Midas, GOLDEN RETRIEVER

Dexter, BELGIAN SHEPHERD

Zoey, KING CHARLES CAVALIER / POODLE MIX

THE DOGS WITH
EYES WIDE OPEN

Abbey

Abbie

Andromache

Bailey

Bailey

Bailey

Barney

Bella

Ben

Bo

Boo

Bosco

Bubba

Butch

Casey-Jane

Daisy

Dayzee

Dexter

Dolly

Donnie

Dozer

Dozer

Dug

Effi

George Gordon Gracie

Grover Hades Hairy

Harley Harrison Harry

Hunter Indy Jeffrey

Jessie Jessie Jet

Kato Kelcie Koda

Kono Levi Lexie

Lexie

Lily

Major

Midas

Miley

Minnie

Mollie Moo

Mr. Scruffy

Muska

Ned

Ollie

Peaches

Pepperoni

Pip

Pixel

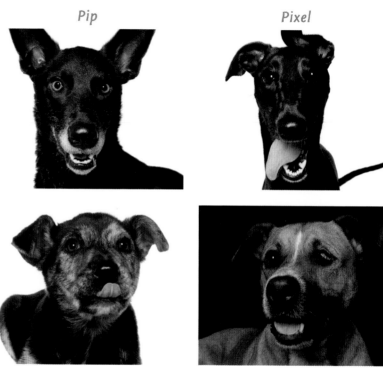

Pluto

Polly

Sam

Sharon Sidney Simon

Staiton Storm Suzi

Sydney Tatu Teddy Bear

Woody Zac Zoey

Acknowledgments

First, I would like to express my gratitude to the wonderful people who visit my studio for portrait photographs of their beloved dogs. You can only capture a Zen Dog if you are photographing an authentically relaxed and happy dog. Every dog in this book was very much loved and adored by their humans and living the best type of life a dog can.

To the Zen Dogs themselves, thank you for "giving" me these sweet images. They make people laugh and smile and are a true gift from you to us.

From HarperOne, I would like to thank my kind and patient editor, Julia Pastore, for sharing your *Zen Dogs* vision with me and for your guidance in crafting this book. Your enthusiasm for *Zen Dogs* from start to finish has been infectious, and I greatly appreciate your dedication to making it happen. Thanks also to the entire HarperCollins team for supporting *Zen Dogs* and to Terry McGrath for the beautiful visual layout and design. I'm proud to be a part of the HarperCollins family.

Thanks to Kate Bratskier, Damon Scheleur, and Lindsay Holmes from The Huffington Post for sharing the Zen Dogs images online and creating a viral sensation. Their kind invitation to write about my work led to the very book you are reading now, and for that I am eternally grateful.

To my valued sponsors, Tamron, Elinchrom, Spider Holster, and Team Digital, thank you for providing me with the tools of the trade and equipment fast enough to capture a split-second Zen Dog blink.

I would like to thank my dear friend and advisor Andrea McNamara for her friendship and direction and for always being on the other end of the line. And to the other half of Houndstooth Studio, Debora Brown, for her unwavering support and keen perusal of my written work—and for always letting me know where the apostrophes go.

Lastly, to my closest furry companions, Pip, Pixel, and Macy; to my new acquaintance, Kingston, from afar; and to all of my other dog friends, thank you for your inspiring daily antics and unconditional love, joy, and . . . Zen.

About Alex Cearns

Alex Cearns is Australia's leading professional pet and wildlife photographer and the creative director of Houndstooth Studio. A philanthropist, author, educator, adventurer, and animal advocate with more than sixty awards and accolades to her name since 2008, she specializes in crafting exquisite animal portraits that intrinsically capture the joy people find in animals. Cearns works tirelessly to make a difference in the lives of rescued animals and provides pro bono photographic services, fundraising projects, and sponsorship to around fifty local, national, and international animal charities, shelters, and sanctuaries. Her photography and philanthropic efforts have been featured in print, broadcast, and digital media worldwide, including The Huffington Post, Bored Panda, *Russian Geographic, Woman's Day,* the *Daily Mail,* BBC Worldwide, the *Daily Telegraph, Photo Review Australia, Wildlife Australia, Dogs Today* magazine, and *Dogs Life* magazine, and in an Australia Post national stamp release. Cearns is the global ambassador for Tamron's Super Performance lens series and an ambassador for Spider Holster. She was also selected by global tour company World Expeditions to be their first professional female wildlife photography tour leader. She lives in Australia with her partner, two rescue dogs, and rescue cat.